dan
moves up 4

dan
moves up

by Paul J. Deegan
illustrated by Harold Henriksen

AMECUS STREET, MANKATO, MINNESOTA

Published by Amecus Street, 123 South Broad Street, P.O. Box 113, Mankato, Minnesota 56001.
Copyright © 1975 by Amecus Street. International copyright reserved in all countries.
No part of this book may be reproduced in any form without written permission from the publisher.
Printed in the United States. Disbributed by Childrens Press, 1224 West Van Buren Street,
Chicago, Illinois 60607.
Library of Congress Numbers: 74-17069   ISBN: 0-87191-406-9
Library of Congress Cataloging in Publication Data
Deegan, Paul J   1937-
Dan moves up.
SUMMARY: Tenth-grader Dan Murphy's game inproves so much that he is
selected for the high school varsity basketball team.
[1. Basketball—Fiction]   I. Henriksen, Harold, illus.   II. Title.
PZ7.D359Dan   [Fic.]   74-17069
ISBN 0-87191-406-9

4444

"You're a coward, Murphy!" the blond-haired boy had said.

"No, it's just not worth it to me," Dan Murphy had replied.

That exchange had taken place a few minutes earlier at the Paradise, a fast-food restaurant where many Pinetown teenagers gathered.

Now Dan was walking home with Jake Tolson on a mild, fall night. Both were 10th graders at Kennedy High School. Neither were yet old enough to have drivers' licenses. One of their parents would have come to pick them up but they had decided, after leaving the restaurant, to walk home.

The boy who had called Dan a coward was John Harris. He was a 10th grader at Roosevelt, the other high school in Pine-town. Dan knew John from playing basket-ball against him in grade school and in ninth grade.

Harris had called Dan a coward be-cause Dan had told him he wasn't interested in going to a beer party. Harris had wanted Dan to join him, two other boys, and two girls in buying a case of beer. Eighteen was the legal age for drinking in the state. One of the other boys was 17 and had obtained a driver's license which said he was 18. He was going to buy the beer. The group then planned to drive into the country to drink it.

"Would you have gone with them if I hadn't been there?" Dan asked Jake.

"Nah, I don't think so," Dan's tall friend and basketball teammate said. "But I was glad you were so definite about not doing it."

"Well, nothing bad will probably come of it," Dan said. "But I want to play basketball more than I want to drink beer, and you know how the coaches feel about drinking and smoking."

"Yeh," Jake said, "they wouldn't take long to decide you couldn't play."

"Thirty seconds, maybe," Dan said with a smile.

"I don't think a beer or two is going to hurt you though," Jake said as the two boys turned onto Trail Avenue which led from downtown to the neighborhood where they both lived.

"I don't think so either," Dan said, "but the rule's there and if you want to play, you're going to have to follow it. We've talked about it at home and my dad thinks it doesn't hurt an athlete to have to sacrifice something. He says it's a way of showing that playing is important to you."

"Besides," Dan continued, "I don't really like beer that much. My dad's always got beer around the house and I can have one if I ask."

"Yeh, me too," Jake said. "I kinda like it, especially on a hot day. But doing it the way those guys are tonight could mean trouble and I don't need that."

"I know that my mom and dad would be disappointed in me if I did something like that," Dan said. "They give me a lot of freedom, but they expect me to use my head. Sometimes I'd like to try things, but I wouldn't want to foul up either. So if a situation looks like it could be trouble, I try to steer away from it."

"Doesn't it make you mad, though, when somebody like Harris gives you a bad time?" Jake asked.

"Sure," Dan said, "but John isn't a bad guy. He just got angry because, when I refused, it made him question what he was going to do. And that's uncomfortable."

"Especially when there are a couple of girls there," Jake said.

"Yeh, that's true," Dan said.

"You know, if I didn't have any friends," Dan continued, "it would probably be a lot harder to say no to what Harris suggested. I like him well enough, but I don't need him for a friend — especially if he doesn't want to respect my decisions."

"Wonder how he'll react the next time you see him," Jake said as he turned to walk toward his house.

"I don't know but we'll find out, I

suppose. See you tomorrow, Jake."

Dan forgot about his encounter with John Harris until the first day of practice for the 10th grade team.

While he was shooting before practice started, he thought to himself: "I'm sure glad I don't have to wonder whether anyone knew I went on a beer party. I can just concentrate on making the team."

The first day of practice for the Kennedy 10th grade team was much different from what it had been the year before. Over 80 boys had tried out for the ninth grade team. This year there were fewer than 25 boys on the floor awaiting the arrival of 10th grade coach Howard Anderson and his assistant.

The coaches had never said that no one could try out for the team if he hadn't been invited. But few boys ever turned up who hadn't been asked because they figured they wouldn't get much of a chance.

Those who had been invited included the members of last year's ninth grade team and a few boys who had transferred to Kennedy from Roosevelt, the other public school in town; from the Catholic high school in Pinetown; or from other communities.

For the first time since he had started playing on teams in the fifth grade, Dan was not really worried about making the team. He wasn't cocky about it, but he knew after his ninth grade year that he could play with anybody his age. Whether he could play well enough to continue as a starter was the only real question in his mind.

Dan had grown an inch or so since the previous basketball season and was over 6 feet, 3 inches. Never exceptionally quick, he knew that his quickness had improved over the summer. His shooting ability, always good, hadn't been harmed by practicing almost every day during vacation. He had shot at the basket in his driveway and played at a park near his house and sometimes in the gym at Oakdale, the grade school in his neighborhood.

Each summer in Pinetown, the gyms at Oakdale and two of the other five grade schools in the city were open three afternoons and three evenings a week. The coaches at

YOU'RE A COWARD MURPHY!

the high schools had asked the school system
to do this several summers earlier. Dan and
Jake Tolson had gone across town a few
times to join kids from other neighborhoods
for pickup games.

Once school had started, Dan shot
in the Kennedy gym almost every day after
classes. Here and during the summer he had

become involved in games with boys on the varsity team. He made some mistakes, but found he could hold his own most of the time. The increased confidence had made him more relaxed as the 10th grade season began.

After three days of practice, Coach Anderson had cut the squad to 17 boys. He said that he would drop two more boys at the end of the week. The 15 who remained would form the 10th grade team.

During that first week, the coaches had been running players at random into the various drills. There was no indication who would be bidding for the starting positions. Jake Tolson, who was now over 6 feet, 6 inches, was figured to be a sure starter. Dan and the other three boys who had started on the ninth grade team figured they would get first chance at the other spots.

On Monday, the squad down to 15 boys, Coach Anderson began working the team in some five-on-five situations. He never said one group was his first choice as starters, but four of the starting five from the ninth grade team were on one side.

They included Jake, Dan, Stan Sterner, and Greg Sims. Jeff Hano, a transfer from Ironridge in the northern part of the state, was the other member of this group. Jeff, 6 feet, 4 inches, had looked good in the first week's drills. He was at the wing spot where John Swanson had played in ninth grade.

Dan and Jake were almost always on the floor together, while Coach Anderson often worked Swanson and other players at the wings and baseline spots in Kennedy's 1-2-2 basic offense.

"Looks like you're going to be playing most of the time," Jake said to Dan a few nights later as they watched the Kennedy varsity football team play.

"Yeh," Dan replied, "I hope so. Even though I'm playing right now, the competition is better this year. There aren't any hamburgers around at all."

"I wish you wouldn't have used that word," Ted said. "I just decided I was hungry."

"I'm cold," Dan said.

It had been a pleasant, sunny day and out on the field, the Kennedy Stags were sweating. The late fall night, though, was becoming chilly, especially when you were just sitting in the stands.

Neither of the boys wanted to leave the game because their friend, Ron Dale, was playing. Only a 10th grader, Ron had made the starting backfield on the varsity.

A halfback, Ron had scored a touchdown tonight on a 12-yard run.

It was one of four touchdowns the Stags had scored. They led the Bensonville team 27-7 with the game midway in the final quarter.

"They aren't having much trouble tonight, are they?" Jake said.

"No, I didn't think they would," Dan replied. "Bensonville has won only three games. But it's good to see Ron doing so well in football."

"He really felt bad when he got dropped in the final cut for the ninth grade basketball team last year," Jake said.

"Yeh, I remember the day," Dan said. "I was glad I didn't see him before practice that day. I didn't know what to say."

"Hey, there's only a minute left to play," Jake said. "Let's start going now."

"Where we going? The Paradise?" Dan asked.

"I suppose so," Jake replied. "If we can get a ride."

The Paradise was about six blocks from Kennedy, but over three miles from

Roosevelt high. The Kennedy football team played their home games at Roosevelt, the older of Pinetown's two high schools. There were no permanent seats or lights at the Kennedy field.

Outside the field, Dan saw Joe Toomey, a neighbor and an 11th grader at Kennedy. Joe had a car.

"Hey, Joe!" Dan shouted. "Are you going to the Paradise? Can we get a ride?"

"Sure," Joe shouted back over the noise of the people leaving the field.

At the Paradise, Dan and Jake slid into a booth where four others were already sitting.

There were two girls, Sandra Brady and Beth Bronson, and two boys, Ted Thompson and Irv Steiner. Sandra, Beth and Irv were also 10th graders at Kennedy.

"Cold out there tonight," Ted said.

"Yeh, that's what I like about basketball," Jake said with a smile. "It never gets cold inside the gym."

"Basketball has started, hasn't it?" Irv asked.

"Yeh, a couple weeks ago," Dan said.

"But several of us have played almost every day since school started."

"And all summer, too," Sandra said.

"Don't you ever get tired of basketball?" Beth asked, looking at Dan and Ted.

"No, not really," Dan replied. "I like it."

"I guess I'd rather do something else once in a while," Ted said, "maybe just lay around even. But if I want to play on the 10th grade team this year, I had to keep practicing."

"Why couldn't you just lay off — say for this year — and then go out for the varsity next year?" Irv asked Ted.

"Nobody would stop me," Ted said, "but I'd fall pretty far behind the others in a year. Then next year the coaches would have to favor the kids that had played this year."

"Besides," Dan said, "nobody makes us play. At least for me, it's just something that I want to do. I enjoy it."

"Maybe if you guys played less basketball, you'd have more time for girls," Beth said.

Irv smiled at Jake, "Tolson seems to be able to fit girls into his schedule."

Beth, who had gone to several movies with Jake since school had started, said, "He can find time, but it would be nice if he could talk about something besides basketball . . . or football . . . or baseball."

After a waitress came and took orders for hamburgers and pop, Irv said, "Well, we can't talk about sports, what else should we try?"

"Hey, I know something I think about sometimes," Jake said. "You know how we study about ecology, how everybody's supposed to be against pollution, and how sometimes kids give older people a bad time about polluting?"

"Well," he continued, "I ran a little bit this summer to stay in shape. And you notice things alongside a road a lot more when you're running than when you're driving. Well, I was really surprised to see all the stuff in the ditches right outside of town. There are beer cans, pop cans, paper cups, and wrappings from food places. And it's not just in the country. There's one hill in

town I ran down sometimes . . ."

"How about up?" Dan interrupted.

"Be quiet," Jake laughed and continued. "Anyway this hill, Longwood Avenue, you should see it! There's the same kind of garbage all alongside of it, too."

"What are you getting at?" Sandra asked. "That despite all the talk about ecology and stuff, nobody's really doing much of anything about it?"

"I think some people are doing things," Irv said. "We won't buy throwaway bottles at our house any more and we sort out our garbage and take the reusable stuff to a recycling center."

"Yeh, Sandra, that's partly what I was thinking," Jake said. "Though Irv's right, too. Some people are trying to cut down on waste. But what I was really thinking was that most of that stuff that I saw thrown in the ditches was probably put there by kids. Not little kids, maybe, but kids old enough to have cars."

"You mean we shouldn't give our parents a bad time unless we can do a better job ourselves?" Beth asked.

"Yeah, I guess so," Jake said.

"Why do you think it's mostly kids doing that?" Irv asked Jake.

"Because it's kids who drive around and drink and eat in their cars. Older people don't do that very often. I'm sure many of them throw stuff out of cars, too. But I think most of the stuff I saw was tossed there by younger people."

"Well, we just proved that we can talk about something besides sports," Sandra said.

"Or boys," Jake added.

"Oh, be quiet," Beth told Jake as the group got up to leave the restaurant.

"Anybody got a ride?" someone asked.

"I'm going to call my dad," Dan said. "We'll give you a ride."

After the last of his four friends had been let off, Dan and Mr. Murphy headed home.

"What did you think of Sandra?" Dan asked suddenly.

"The girl in the brown coat?"

"Yeh."

"Gee, I don't know," Mr. Murphy said. "She's nice looking and friendly but I didn't really get any chance to form an impression of her. Why?"

"I was just wondering," Dan said.

Dan didn't say anymore but whenever he saw Sandra in school during the next few weeks, he always smiled and said hello.

After school, he didn't have time to think about much except basketball. It was the week before the first game for the 10th graders and Coach Anderson was working the team harder than he had earlier.

The 10th grade team played on the same nights as the varsity. The 10th graders would play first, usually starting at 6 p.m. The varsity game would follow. This would be the pattern through the season, both for games at home and away.

Thursday, the day before the first game with Harwood, Coach Anderson ran the team through what would be their warm-up drills before a game, had the players shoot 25 free throws each, and ended practice after 40 minutes.

Dan wasn't especially nervous the

next night. When the team came on the floor for warm-up drills, there were not many people in the stands. "Just like practice," Dan told himself. He also noticed that the Harwood team was not as big as the Kennedy 10th graders.

Coach Anderson had noticed, too. After naming Dan along with Tolson, Sterner, Sims, and Hano as the starters, the coach looked at Dan. "Murphy, let's see if we can't get that ball inside right away. Either hit Tolson yourself or set up so Sterner or Hano can get it in the hole."

Then he said to everyone, "Let's work those boards now. You've got the size, let's take advantage of it."

As Dan walked onto the floor for the opening tip-off, he noticed that one of the Kennedy 10th grade cheerleaders was Sandra Brady.

Jake controlled the tip and after the first few minutes, Kennedy controlled the game. They were making good use of their height advantage.

After Dan had made his first shot of the night, there had been no more first-game nervousness for him. Dan scored 16 points in the first quarter and a half before Coach Anderson removed the starters for the rest of the first half.

Kennedy won the game by 22 points and Dan had 24 points after sitting out almost all of the final quarter. When the game ended, the cheerleaders came on the floor to congratulate the players and Sandra ran up to Dan. He was surprised, but glad. When she said, "Nice game, Dan. You were great!", all that he could think of to say was, "Yeh, thanks." He did give her a quick smile; then he hurried off the floor to the locker room.

After the game, Dan sat for a few minutes with his parents, who had watched the game. "You all played well, especially for a first game," Mr. Murphy said. "You really shot well, Dan, and you got the ball inside."

"Coach told us to work the ball inside. They didn't move well on defense and it was easy for me to get open. Mr. Anderson noticed this right away and told me to put it up whenever I could."

The 10th graders won five more games and then lost by two points at Dellwood. Dan had a bad night shooting and Jake got into foul trouble. Still, the Kennedy team had a chance to tie the game when Dan took a jump shot from 12 feet with five seconds to play. It didn't go down.

Dan was disappointed but he had been playing long enough now to know these things were going to happen. He thought about what he could have done differently as he lay in bed that night, then forgot about it.

The 10th graders won a three-day holiday tournament in their own gym, then added another victory after school resumed. The next game was the first of the two meetings with Roosevelt. This one would be at Roosevelt.

Dan hadn't thought about John Harris since the first day of practice. During the week before the Roosevelt game, he found himself thinking about Harris quite often. All the Kennedy players wanted to have a good night against Roosevelt. Dan especially wanted to play well.

The coaches felt the game was special, too. They prepared a 1-3-1 zone with Dan out on the point, just as he was on offense. It would be the first time that Dan or his teammates would play a zone. The Kennedy coaches thought Dan would create problems for the Roosevelt guards, three inches shorter. The coaches also knew Roosevelt would not expect them to play a zone. They had played only man-to-man so far.

Dan worked hard in practice. He knew that one of the guards in the two-guard Roosevelt offense would be John Harris.

The night of the game, unlike most game nights, the stands were beginning to fill rapidly by the time the 10th grade game started. The hometown rivalry brought fans out early to make sure they got seats. Both teams were nervous and conscious of the crowd.

Kennedy turned the ball over after controlling the opening tip. Dan and his teammates went into their zone as John Harris brought the ball down floor for the Roosevelt 10th graders.

Dan played high, well above the top

of the free throw circle. The Roosevelt players didn't immediately recognize the zone and started moving in their man-to-man pattern. When the forward on the left side tried to come up, no Kennedy player came with him. There were three Roosevelt men within a few feet of each other and the ball. They all looked confused.

Harris had the ball and began dribbling back toward the center of the court. Dan cut him off and Harris whipped a hurried pass underneath.

Jake Tolson moved quickly to cut off the bad pass. As soon as Dan had seen that the ball would probably be intercepted, he began moving down court. Tolson grabbed the ball, noticed Dan was moving, and fired it. The pass bounced ahead of Dan. He controlled it and dribbled in for an easy lay-up.

The Roosevelt coaches were standing, signaling for a time-out before their players could put the ball in play.

After the time-out, Roosevelt set up in a zone offense, but it was obvious they weren't used to playing against a zone. However, Harris and both Roosevelt forwards were good ball players. They began to move the ball better as the game continued. Dan worked hard at chasing the guards when the ball was out front. Harris had only one shooting opportunity in the first period, a shot which he missed.

The Roosevelt forwards, though, were shooting well and keeping their team in the game. Both teams had overcome their early nervousness. Dan's determination was also evident when Kennedy had the ball. He wasn't hurrying his moves too much, but he was forcing openings and shooting when they were there. He had four baskets in the first quarter and had hit Tolson and Sterner with good passes which led to baskets.

Early in the second quarter with Kennedy leading 16-10, Harris got a quick return pass from a forward and put up a jumper just as Dan got back to him. Dan couldn't stop his movement and hit Harris' arm just after he released the shot. The ball went through, the referee called a foul, and Harris made the free throw. Kennedy's lead was cut to three points.

Dan was angry, but in a good way. He was learning that mistakes were part of the game. He wasn't happy about reacting too late, but the mistake didn't cause him to lose control. He was just more determined to play well.

He brought the ball into the front court and saw Jeff Hano move up to set a pick for him. He switched his dribble to his left hand. Harris, who was guarding him, moved over to cut him off. Suddenly, he switched the ball back to his right hand, drove hard for two steps and went up for his jumper. Swish! Kennedy's lead went to five points.

Sterner batted away a Roosevelt pass at the other end of the court. When he brought the ball back to his offensive end, Dan passed to Sterner on the right point. Sterner fed the ball into the middle to Tolson and Dan broke down the lane on the pass. He had his man beat. Tolson bounced the ball off to Dan, who went up and scored the lay-up. The Roosevelt center had left Tolson to cover Dan, but he was too late and crashed into Dan as he put the ball off the glass. Dan went to the free throw line and had the three-point play back.

In the next few minutes, Dan scored three more baskets and Kennedy had a 12-point lead. Roosevelt cut the margin to eight at half time, but Dan kept the hot hand in the second half. He had 26 points when Coach Anderson took out the first string with two minutes to play and Kennedy ahead by 15.

The Kennedy varsity players, waiting at the locker room door to go on the floor, congratulated Dan and his teammates as they noisily entered the room.

Dan had sought out John Harris after the game to shake his hand. John didn't have much to say. Dan hadn't expected much of a conversation.

In the shower, Dan began to relax, content with the feeling that only victory and playing well can bring an athlete.

Mr. Murphy was all smiles when Dan talked to him for a few minutes after the game. "That's the best I ever saw you play, Dan," his father said.

"I just hope I can keep it up," Dan said.

Jake Tolson came up to where Dan and his parents were talking and Dan and Jake left to find a seat to watch the varsity game.

Early in the second quarter of the varsity game, which Kennedy was controlling by a small margin, Kennedy's point man, Marv Libby, got hammered on a lay-up attempt. He fell hard on the wooden floor. He reached out to grab his leg and then fell back again, obviously in pain.

Libby, a 12th grader, went to the locker room and didn't return with the varsity team for the second half. Kennedy came from behind in the last two minutes to win the game by three points.

When Dan was leaving his homeroom for his first class on the following Monday morning, his homeroom teacher handed him a note. Moving into the hall to go to his first class, Dan opened the note. It read: "Please meet me in the coaches' office at 11:45." It was signed by Mr. Anderson.

Dan had no idea why the coach wanted to see him in the middle of the day.

ON THE VARSITY TEAM

He couldn't recall doing anything to create a problem, so he didn't worry about the summons. But he was curious.

When Dan got to the coaches' office at 11:45 that morning, Mr. Anderson was there but so was Al McNulty, the varsity head basketball coach.

"Hi, Dan," Mr. Anderson said.

"Hello, son," Mr. McNulty said. "Please sit down for a minute."

"Mr. McNulty wants to talk to you," Mr. Anderson told Dan.

"Dan," the varsity coach said, "I want to bring you up to the varsity team, starting today."

The excitement rose in Dan and he could feel the sweat beginning to form under his arms.

"I haven't done this very often at Kennedy," Mr. McNulty continued, "because it's a large enough school that I usually have plenty of juniors and seniors who can play ball. I also believe it's better for a boy to play on a regular basis for the 10th grade team than on a part-time basis for the varsity. He improves more and it helps his confidence.

"But Libby broke his ankle Friday and the doctors don't think he'll play again this year. After watching you play against Roosevelt and talking with Coach Anderson, we think you can help the varsity right now," Coach McNulty told Dan. "You're big enough and you have improved a good deal since ninth grade — more than I had expected."

"I don't know what to say, coach," Dan said. "I hadn't even thought about playing on the varsity until next year. But I'm sure going to try to take advantage of the opportunity you've given me."

Dan left the coaches' office in somewhat of a daze. Since moving up to the varsity was a real surprise, something he had not even considered, he felt rather numb.

He wanted to tell somebody, so he decided to find Jake. Otherwise, he planned to keep quiet and hope for the best.

Dan was on the varsity basketball team at Kennedy High School. His goal was realized earlier than he had ever thought possible.

CREATIVE EDUCATION

DAN MURPHY SPORTS STORIES

56123